# *Roger Oxley*

## LOOKS AT

# AUSTRALIAN TREES

# *Roger Oxley*
## LOOKS AT
# AUSTRALIAN TREES

## *Foreword by Ian McNamara*

an
ABC
BOOK

Published by ABC Books for the
AUSTRALIAN BROADCASTING CORPORATION
GPO Box 9994 Sydney NSW 2001

*First published 1993*

National Library of Australia
Cataloguing-in-Publication entry
Oxley, Roger,
    Roger Oxley looks at Australian trees.

    ISBN 0 7333 0265 3.

    1. Trees-Australian. I. Australian Broadcasting
    Corporation. II. Title.
582.160994

Front Cover: River Red Gum
Back Cover: Banksia

Photographs of Wild Orange and Red Cedar by Ross Sawtell.
All other photographs by Roger Oxley

*Designed by Deborah Brash/Brash Design*
*Set in 11/13½pt Schneidler by Midland Typesetters,*
*Maryborough, Victoria.*
*Printed and bound in Australia by*
*APG, Maryborough, Victoria.*

5-1695

9  8  7  9  6  5  4  3  2  1

# Contents

# Alphabetical List of Plants

# Foreword

Roger has been the tree correspondent for *Australia All Over* since about 1987 and has brought an awareness and appreciation of trees to listeners on Sunday mornings. I know that because of the heaps of letters and phone calls I get on the subject. His story on pepper trees prompted stacks of letters from people and it seems just about everybody has a story to tell which they can relate to pepper trees. Similarly, Roger's story on mallee back in 1988, in which he mentioned that the depletion in mallee fowl numbers was partly due to feral cats, resulted in a deluge of letters.

This book is different to other tree books in that Roger has used a mixture of factual, anecdotal and personal knowledge and experiences to talk about his favourite subject.

Roger is keenly aware of the environment, how it works and what is happening to it. If you pull up beside the road anywhere you like, he can introduce you to the intricacies of Nature—whether it's the trees or the grasses or the delicate relationship between the plants and animals that happen to live there. He can make a trip interesting. It's amazing what you can see when the obvious is pointed out. All too often we can't see the forest for the trees so to speak.

It's a pleasure for me to introduce you to his book. Roger's love of trees and concern for the environment are something that I equally share and if we don't look after our unique countryside we'll surely go down the gurgler.

*Ian M'Namara*

# Introduction

Australia has been separated from other lands for something like sixty million years and during this time has slowly but surely been drifting north. The climate has not always been as it is today. It has fluctuated through warm and humid times when most of the land was covered by rainforests to several glacial periods when permanent snow and ice shaped the high country of New South Wales, Victoria and Tasmania. There have been periods when the sea covered vast areas of land. In more recent times the climate has become more arid. Rainforests are confined to areas of eastern Australia and the vegetation over most of the country is now dominated by *Eucalyptus* and *Acacia*.

The Australian vegetation as we see it today has largely been shaped by Aboriginal use of fire over at least 40 000 years. Most of our plants have adapted to or are able to cope with fire in some way. The heat from bushfires cracks the hard wattle seeds so that they can absorb moisture and germinate and it causes banksias to release their seeds. Even our tallest eucalypt, the majestic mountain ash, depends on fire for its continued survival. Fire is a natural part of the environment.

Australia has a deplorable record of taking care of its land and resources. In the relatively short time since European occupation we have managed to clear and burn about three-quarters of our rainforests and get rid of two-thirds of our original tree cover. Across most of the rural areas, especially in the more settled regions, the population of trees is becoming older and older. All too often the only trees remaining in paddocks are geriatric and in the process of decay. Grazing and cultivation prevent any regeneration. In some places it is only along roadsides, railways and in reserves where any semblance of the former vegetation can be found.

However, there are stacks of trees that are hundreds of years old. They have not succumbed to the axe or bulldozer and have withstood the ravages of fire, storm and even white ants. There are trees bearing scars left by Aborigines who cut off sheets of bark for their canoes and coolamons. There are trees which bear explorers' inscriptions and there are trees which testify to the first surveyors.

Trees are the largest and oldest living things on Earth. They are things of beauty and are the dominant feature of our landscapes. They have captured the imagination of poets, authors, painters, songwriters and photographers and are an integral part of our folklore, heritage and way of life. Trees are essential for the health and well-being of the land itself. Without them our landscapes become degraded and unproductive—the natural balance becomes upset.

Back in 1987 the *Australia All Over, Volume 1* record was released. One song on it, *Wild and Free*, written and sung by John Broomhall, contained the names of sixty or so trees in its lyrics. This song prompted me to begin writing to *Australia All Over* on the subject of trees and in this book each story is printed essentially as read by Ian McNamara on Sunday mornings.

# Plane Tree

*Platanus acerifolia*

Some towns and cities seem to be synonymous with certain kinds of trees. In fact many towns hold some sort of annual festival based on a tree theme. Grafton with its jacaranda festival is a well-known example.

Other towns and cities are characterised by their trees even though they might not be formally recognised. Take plane trees for instance. Richmond, on the outskirts of Sydney, has a fine avenue of these trees, and plane trees give Melbourne's city streets their cool, leafy appearance in summer. However Narrandera, in southern New South Wales, would have to take first prize for its beautiful plane trees. Here they have grown to an immense size and provide copious shade to many streets during the heat of summer.

The plane tree, or more correctly the London plane, is a cross between an Asian and an American species and is probably the most commonly planted street tree in the world. It is a quick grower, copes with living in smog-laden air and doesn't seem to mind using water that is full of all the contaminants that wash from dirty asphalt roads and footpaths.

Like so many other street trees they are sometimes planted in places that are unsuitable. All too often they have to be severely cut back so they won't foul overhead power lines. Such drastic pruning doesn't appear to worry them and they soon respond in the following spring by growing new branches.

As is the case with so many of the northern hemisphere's trees, plane trees are deciduous and shed their large leaves in autumn. These leaves are indeed large. I have measured one fifty centimetres across (that's about twenty inches in the old language) on a tree growing at my place. This isn't the norm, though; most leaves are smaller.

The problem with deciduous trees of course is that they make a mess when the leaves fall. Steps, paths, patios, gardens and lawns disappear under a thick layer of leaves and have to be continually cleaned up.

The flowers are rather inconspicuous but form round, ball-shaped fruits which hang down on long stems. Each fruit contains hundreds of very sharp pointed seeds which are a real hazard to bare feet. They even go through your thongs.

One of the most attractive things about plane trees is the bark, which flakes off, giving the trunk and branches a mottled appearance with colours ranging from a creamy white to grey and olive green.

Anyone contemplating growing a plane tree should be careful where it is planted. If too near a house the leaves and seeds will clog up gutters and the roots can lift up paths and choke out garden beds. However they are easy to grow, create A-grade shade and once established are extremely hardy.

# Dieback

One of the most visible symptoms of the land degradation that is spreading like a cancerous growth across much of rural Australia is dieback—the death of our native trees. It has reared its head in many places— from the northern tablelands around Armidale in New South Wales (perhaps the most infamous area) to the southern tablelands, from Goulburn to Cooma. It's not confined only to New South Wales; it occurs in much of the south west of Western Australia, in South Australia, Tasmania, Victoria and Queensland. In the main it seems to be associated with areas that have been substantially cleared and used for some sort of improved agriculture.

The latest region to have succumbed is the southern Riverina of New South Wales where massive dieback is causing grave concern, especially among the rural community.

Dieback is the slow deterioration in the health of our trees which more often than not ultimately leads to their death. Most commonly the eucalypts are the ones that suffer and not necessarily only a single tree or two. Whole communities can be wiped out.

Dieback, or rural tree decline as some euphemistically put it, is not caused by a single factor. A multitude of things interacting in a complex way are responsible. Clearing and loss of the general tree cover, loss of the shrub and grass understorey, massive inputs of fertilisers and pesticides, insect predation, poor irrigation practices, rising water tables, salinity and grazing all come into play.

The alarm bells are ringing, nature is calling for help. We have upset the balance of things. For all too long ecology has suffered under the blade of the economic bulldozer. Short-term monetary gain has led to long-term environmental and social problems. What is required is a change in the attitude to the way we manage our land and its resources.

Don't get me wrong. Of course we need our grain, our timber, our cattle and sheep as well as the stuff that grows on their backs. But we must learn to live in harmony with our environment, not exploit it. Our land must be treated in a sustainable way so that it will continue to provide us with its harvest.

Just as there is no single cause, there is no single cure for dieback. There is no quick fix. Planting new trees will alleviate the problem to some extent but it is the underlying causes that must be addressed. It is no good merely treating the symptoms. We have to go to the roots of the problem if we are to be fair dinkum. It requires a serious and concerted effort by all of us, individuals, land-care groups and governments alike. The recovery process will be slow and in some cases will be hard. The costs will have to be borne by us all and will be economic as well as social.

# Grevillea

*Grevillea* spp.

Grevilleas belong to the Proteaceae family which also includes the banksias, waratahs, hakeas and the macadamia. The Proteaceae appear to have originated in Gondwanaland well over 100 million years ago. Today plants of this family are found in South Africa, South America and parts of south east Asia as well as Australia.

Grevilleas, or spider flowers as they are sometimes known, occur in a wide range of environments, from rainforests to alpine regions and even deserts. They are all woody plants and vary from small prostrate shrubs to tall trees. There are about 250 different kinds in Australia with a few more in New Guinea, New Caledonia and the Celebes.

They are grown for a variety of reasons and make good hedges. No self-respecting native garden should be without at least one grevillea. The silky oak is perhaps the tallest of all the grevilleas and has been planted throughout Australia in gardens, parks and as a street tree. The roads leading into Tamworth are lined with hundreds of silky oaks which make a fine display in the early summer every year.

One fairly common grevillea found over much of the dry inland is beefwood. Its dark furrowed bark and long thin leathery leaves up to half a metre in length make it a rather attractive tree which can grow up to twelve metres high. Its typical grevillea flowers are a creamy yellow colour and provide food for a wide range of nectar-feeding birds and insects.

The tree gets its common name because of the resemblance of its freshly cut wood to that of raw beef.

It makes excellent fence posts, is easily split and was used to make roof shingles in the pioneering days. A resin derived from the roots provided the Aborigines with a cementing material to fix stone implements to wooden handles.

The beefwood standing beside John Poole's grave at Depot Glen near Milparinka in north western New South Wales bears the inscription 'J.P. 1845'. Poole was second in command to the explorer Charles Sturt and this simple epitaph, carved by Sturt, remains quite legible today. Beefwood is certainly a long-lived tree.

# Berrigan

## *Eremophila longifolia*

A very common shrub or small tree which grows in the drier parts of Australia is berrigan. Like nearly all of our native plants it has a number of common names— emu bush, because its fruit are eaten by emus, and native plum tree, because of the purple colour of the fruit.

Berrigan is an Aboriginal name and is one of the 100 or so kinds of *Eremophila* which are found only in Australia. The name *eremophila*, is derived from the Greek words *eremos* (desert) and *philos* (love of).

Most are shrubs, occasionally some grow to small trees. They have attractive tubular, fuchsia-like flowers ranging in all colours from white to red, blue, purple, yellow and even green. The flowers attract nectar-feeding birds and insects—the green flowers on some are interesting because they are pollinated by moths during the night time. The usual form is a shrub, often growing in thickets around the parent plant. This becomes particularly noticeable when it suckers following fire or some other disturbance, such as slashing.

Berrigan grows on a wide range of soil types and although its flowers are not as spectacular as some of its relatives, it is a useful plant for growing as an ornamental in gardens and parks. Like most other eremophilas propagation is usually achieved by cuttings as the seed is difficult to germinate.

In many parts of Australia's interior eremophilas have become so thick that pasture grasses are unable to grow and this has led to a marked decline in the stock-carrying capacity of the country. Berrigan is not as bad in this respect as some of its cousins because both sheep and cattle find the foliage to their liking and a pronounced browse line is visible on mature plants. Even in moderately grazed paddocks young plants may be difficult to find because they are constantly eaten by stock but if the paddock is left ungrazed for a while berrigan will sucker profusely and become very thick.

# Dillon Bush

*Nitraria billardieri*

Most people would never have heard of dillon bush, or nitre bush as it is sometimes known. This is not surprising because most of the time it doesn't have a lot going for it even though it is quite common. For miles and miles along the stockroutes, creek and river frontages and flogged-out paddocks across much of the dry country it thrives. It copes well, even during severe droughts when other plants have shrivelled and blown away.

Dillon bush is a large, dense, compact, ground-hugging shrub that can grow well over a couple of metres high and more than six metres in diameter.

There is only one species in Australia, in fact it's the only species in the Southern Hemisphere. To the casual observer the bushes are often thought to be dead. Not so. Dillon bush is one of our few native plants that are deciduous, as it loses most of its leaves during winter. However, come spring new leaves appear and the bushes really start to green up.

Every now and then dillon bushes display a mass of red, purple and yellow fruit because of the droughty conditions in the late spring and early summer when the bushes are flowering. This may seem rather strange but apparently if too much rain falls during this period insects have a hard time feeding and the flowers miss out on being pollinated.

The brightly coloured fruit are a favourite food of emus and during the summer they eat them by the millions. The success and spread of dillon bush owes much to the humble emu. Undigested seeds within the fruit that have been eaten germinate much better than those that haven't been eaten. It appears that if it weren't for emus dillon bushes would not be so common and widespread.

Ripe fruit were also eagerly sought by Aborigines and there are indications that the fruit on whole bushes was stripped and eaten on the spot. There would certainly have been a feast as individual bushes can bear many thousands of fruit in summer.

The dense, compact nature of dillon bushes makes them ideal places for a wide range of animals to seek shelter and protection. This is especially important in areas where trees are few and far between. Large bushes invariably contain a system of tunnels and pathways where you may find everything from rabbits and foxes to kangaroos, reptiles and various ground dwelling birds.

The intimate relationship between climate, insects and emus and the life and times of dillon bush is just another example of the complex pattern of nature.

# Biddy Bush

## Cassinia aculeata

It's not very often that a native plant has the dubious distinction of being included on the noxious weed list. However, one such plant is biddy bush, also known as sifton bush or Chinese-shrub.

It is of particular concern on the tablelands and western slopes of New South Wales as well as in Victoria where it has overrun thousands and thousands of acres of grazing country. In New South Wales alone well over one million acres have been infested. Problems with biddy bush are not new. In parts of central Victoria it was declared a noxious weed just on 100 years ago!

Biddy bush is a small evergreen shrub which grows to a couple of metres high. It is distinctive by its masses of small brownish flowers and by its very strong curry smell. It's a wonder that it hasn't ever been used as a substitute for curry because there's no shortage of it. I have no idea how it got its common name of biddy bush or sifton bush but its other common name, Chinese-shrub, originated from the gold-rush days. Apparently Chinese miners used it to thatch the roofs of their huts.

Farmers around Orange will know of biddy bush because it is very common in the district. Following the 1982 drought it came up *en masse*. The problem is now so acute that a concerted research effort has been mounted to look for cheap and effective methods of control. Herbicides, slashing and burning as well as biological control are all being looked at.

The situation with biddy bush is very similar to that encountered further to the west in New South Wales where other native shrubs, the so-called woody weeds, have run amok over vast areas of grazing country.

We all know that many plants that have been introduced into Australia have become noxious weeds. One of the main reasons for this is that they were introduced without their natural enemies. There was no biological control. However, it is interesting to ask why a native plant has become noxious.

The answer lies in how we have mismanaged the land. We have introduced sheep and cattle and have ruthlessly overgrazed and overcleared the country. Fire, once an integral part of the system, has been eliminated, or, at best, its frequency and intensity have been drastically altered. We have added huge amounts of fertilisers to soil that was inherently poor in nutrients.

Our native plants have responded to the rape of their realm in many ways. Some have been drastically reduced or even eliminated, unable to cope with these sudden changes. Others, like biddy bush, have found things to their liking and have undergone a massive population explosion.

# River Red Gum

*Eucalyptus camaldulensis*

What do the Murray, the Darling, the Murrumbidgee, the Todd, the Barcoo, the Fitzroy and the Gascoyne Rivers have in common? The answer is the river red gum, the most widely distributed of all the eucalypts. In fact this tree can be found along virtually all watercourses in every State in mainland Australia. It is absent only from the southern parts of Western Australia, the Nullarbor Plain and east of the Great Dividing Range from Cape York to Victoria.

The tree varies in form and growth habit but reaches its best development along the lower reaches of the Murray and Murrumbidgee River systems where extensive forests occupy seasonally inundated floodplains. These forests are the centre of an important timber industry and numerous timber mills cut logs for heavy construction work, railway sleepers, fencing and many other uses. The dark red coloured wood polishes to a high gloss and is used for parquetry, ornaments and furniture.

In the early days before the advent of motorised transport, logs were carted from the forests in bullock wagons, loaded onto barges on the Murray and transported to sawmills. Unlike some of the softwood logging operations in North America, logs could not be floated downstream because river red gum wood is so heavy and dense.

The river boats which plied the rivers in the middle of last century played a major role in establishing the woodcutting industry. These steamers required large amounts of wood to fuel their furnaces and great stacks of wood were established along the river banks at regular intervals. The depletion of trees along the river edges during this period probably led to the accelerated erosion and undercutting of the river banks. Nowadays, there are strict regulations and the removal or cutting of trees in the vicinity of creeks and rivers requires special permits.

The river red gum can grow to an immense size, especially where roots can have permanent access to a good supply of moisture. The trunk of larger trees can grow to over four metres in diameter and individuals with butts of three metres are commonplace. These majestic trees living on inland streams are a favourite subject for painters and photographers. The roots and fallen limbs close to the water's edge provide a preferred habitat for fish, especially the wily Murray cod. The hollows in the upper branches provide shelter and safe nesting sites for many kinds of birds including parrots, galahs and cockatoos.

The bark provided Aboriginal canoes. These so-called 'canoe trees' can be seen in many places and are easily recognised by the large scar created by the removal of the bark.

It goes without saying that the river red gum's uses are numerous. It makes excellent firewood, is used for charcoal production and more recently has been planted in the fight against salinity. Young trees are quick growing, pump water out of the soil and so help lower the water table. Trees only two years old can remove up to seventeen litres of water each day.

There is no doubt that the river red gum has been, and will continue to be, of immense social, ecological and economic benefit to both man and animals.

# Saltbush

*Atriplex* spp.

Without a doubt the most unattractive plant mentioned in John Broomhall's *Wild and Free* would have to be the saltbush.

There are about forty kinds of saltbush in Australia, generally confined to the southern half of the continent. They grow from the coast to the dry inland areas. Saltbushes are small, often straggly shrubs—many only growing to less than twenty centimetres high. The tallest one, however, oldman saltbush, can grow to above three metres. Some saltbushes are annuals but the most important ones are perennial and may live for many years. The dull green-grey leaves generally contain high amounts of salt and, to compensate for this, sheep eating the plant require large amounts of good fresh water.

Saltbush occupies extensive areas across Australia, from the Nullarbor Plain through South Australia to the Riverine Plain in south western New South Wales.

The Riverine Plain was the first extensive saltbush area to be exploited by the squatters some 150 years ago. Initially stock were grazed along the rivers where water was available but with the advent of fencing and permanent watering points away from the rivers, sheep could be grazed over the entire area year round. Those early days saw the country suffer from overgrazing and there are now large areas devoid of saltbush. However many graziers are attempting to reintroduce these plants with somewhat mixed success.

Australia's economy owes much to the saltbush plains of the Riverina for it was here that the Peppin merinos had their origin. These merinos were bred to cope with the harsh conditions of Australia and today about eighty-five per cent of the nation's flock is derived from the Peppin flock that evolved during the 1860s.

The saltbush plains around here are seemingly endless: great flat expanses of country broken only by occasional trees growing along drainage lines. The country appears so flat that I reckon you can see the curvature of the earth! These plains are very monotonous for the traveller. Landmarks are the exception rather than the rule and names like 'One-tree plain', 'Dead man's clump' and 'Sixteen mile gums' attest to this.

The leaves of some saltbushes may be used as a substitute for spinach. The explorer, Sir Thomas Mitchell, found that after removing most of the salt by boiling in a couple of changes of water and then boiling again for an hour the leaves made 'a tender and palatable vegetable somewhat resembling spinach'.

# Pepper Tree

## Schinus areira

You either love them or you don't. They are one of the most common trees of country towns and homestead gardens and are invariably found next to the old outside dunny, beside the machinery shed, around the yards and more often than not line either side of the drive leading to the house. One of their most favoured environments is alongside country pub verandahs. They provide excellent shade for the dogs, the chooks, the sheep, the old battered Toyota ute and even a cool spot to hang your waterbag. Unfortunately, they also offer spots for mossies.

This tree, of course, is the pepper tree.

Contrary to popular belief, the pepper tree is not native to Australia but hails from Peru in South America and was introduced here via California sometime last century, possibly by gold-seeking immigrants during the 1850s.

It gets its common name from the masses of small pink-red berries the female tree produces in autumn once flowering has ceased. In the past these berries have been dried and ground and used as a substitute for true pepper.

The pepper tree is a wide-spreading evergreen tree with long, dark-green compound leaves which droop down from the small branches. It is quick-growing and is drought-hardy and resistant to insect pests. However, despite these attributes for survival, it has not invaded the countryside to any great extent as have many other introduced trees. Where small clumps or isolated trees are growing in the middle of nowhere they usually denote the site of former habitation. They are often the sole remaining clue that on that spot there was once a farmhouse, a pub or even a small town.

They don't seem to be grown as commonly nowadays as they were once. They are out of fashion. The reason has probably something to do with the current notion that everything has to be native or else it's no good. The poor old pepper tree is much maligned and often regarded as environmentally unfriendly. However, having said that, there is at least one firm of landscape architects in Melbourne which has recently planted rows of pepper trees in an avenue for a new development.

The pepper tree even looks like a native tree and is just as much a part of our rural landscape as the gum tree. Growing up in the country and pepper trees are somehow synonymous. There would hardly be one country kid who has not had some special attachment to, or memories of, their favourite pepper tree.

# Wilga and Wild Orange

*Geijera parviflora*
*Capparis mitchellii*

Two trees commonly occurring in the drier western half of New South Wales and Queensland are wilga and wild orange. Both are included in John Broomhall's *Wild and Free*.

Wilga grows to around nine metres and has a large, rounded, dense canopy with masses of small white flowers during spring. It is one of the most useful and attractive native trees growing in this grazing country. The leaves of some wilgas provide good feed for sheep and it is common to see an even browse line on some trees while other trees nearby are left ungrazed. The reason for this is unknown.

Wilga is an excellent shade and shelter tree. All kinds of animals, from sheep to kangaroos, feral pigs and goats can be found under its shade during the hot summer months. Wilgas also provide a favoured site for bower birds to construct their bower. I have often seen these bowers under wilgas with the bird's collection of brightly coloured objects ranging from ripe red quandong fruit to the ubiquitous pull tops from drink cans.

Wild orange, or bumbil as it is known in Queensland, occurs in similar country to wilga and grows to about 6 metres. It gets its name from the fruit, about 5 cm in diameter, which it produces. Aborigines are reputed to have eaten the fruit but it has an unpleasant taste and is often infested with grubs of white butterflies. The leaves of wild oranges are avidly sought by sheep, cattle and goats, making it an excellent fodder tree.

Mature trees provide good shade but young plants are thorny, scrambling shrubs which only later develop a main trunk and grow into a tree form. Its wood is hard and has been used for making tobacco pipes.

Both these trees, the wilga and wild orange, are attractive and useful and as such should be protected wherever possible.

# Yarran and Cooba

*Acacia homalophylla*
*Acacia salicina*

There are half a dozen kinds of wattles or acacias mentioned in JB's song *Wild and Free*, and yarran and cooba are two of them. Both are fairly small to medium sized trees with yarran found in the semi-arid country of New South Wales from approximately the Murray in the south to Queensland in the north. Cooba has a greater natural range and occurs in all the mainland states.

Yarran is the smaller of the two trees and is often confused with myall because of its similar appearance. When young, yarran is usually multi-stemmed but soon develops a single trunk and a dense bushy crown and becomes quite a handsome tree which provides good shade for stock. More often than not yarran occurs in dense thickets in areas that receive localised run-off after periods of rain. Sometimes these yarran flats become so thick that nothing else can grow and it may be necessary to thin out the area to encourage the growth of grasses. However, like some other acacias, yarran will sucker if cut down and this may only exacerbate the problem.

Its timber is very hard and heavy and has a variety of uses including fenceposts, cabinet-making and firewood. The Aborigines prized yarran for making boomerangs and spears; in fact one of its common names is spearwood.

Cooba has several common names too. One of the most widely used is native willow which alludes to its drooping willow-like branches and leaves and hence its resemblance to the ubiquitous weeping willows so common along many creeks and rivers. In South Australia it is known as broughton willow and in Queensland as doolan.

Cooba is mostly found along watercourses and under favourable conditions grows to twenty metres, especially in the northern part of its range in Queensland. It is a relatively fast-growing tree which invariably reproduces vegetatively from root suckers. This suckering has value in stabilizing river banks but in other situations its tendency to form thickets may present problems in localized areas.

Cooba can be planted in the semi-arid country for shade, shelter and ornamental purposes. Like other acacias its wood is dark and heavy and has been used for making furniture and, in the early days, cart shafts and bullock yokes. Aborigines used the bark to poison fish in waterholes and the wood to make boomerangs.

# Algae

The latest ecological disaster to rear its ugly head is the population explosion of blue-green algae in many of our rivers, lakes and dams. The algae produce toxins which are lethal to stock and cause severe reactions in humans. Algae-laden water is unfit for consumption.

These algal blooms are caused by massive amounts of nutrients finding their way into the watercourses. The main source of these nutrients includes fertilisers and chemicals which have been applied to agricultural land as well as sewerage effluent from towns along rivers.

Usually stagnant or low river levels and flows are a prerequisite for the growth of large algal blooms. When these conditions coincide with nutrient input then we have the perfect recipe for the growth of the algae and the death of our waterways.

To this can be added a whole host of other man-induced disasters and devastation: wind and water erosion of our fragile topsoils, dryland and irrigation salinity, soil structure decline, soil acidity, loss of native plants and animals, pollution of our beaches . . . the list goes on.

It has been suggested that the Darling River needs flushing out in order to get rid of the algae and dilute the nutrient concentration in the water. This may well be a solution—at least in the short term. However, the logical follow-on from this is that it may give impetus to the push to divert the flow of the coastal rivers of northern New South Wales into the upper Darling catchments—another Snowy Mountains Scheme if you like.

With such a scenario there would be excess water diverted down the Darling and so intensive irrigation schemes would spring up all along the river. You wouldn't need a crystal ball to know what would happen then. There would be large-scale land degradation in the form of clearing and levelling, the inevitable irrigation salinity along with the simultaneous destruction of the remaining trees and wildlife habitats.

Although governments are spending many millions of dollars in an effort to combat our deteriorating environment we cannot leave it solely to them to fix everything up. More often than not, opportunistic, economic and political gains have taken precedence. We have raped our land and its resources under the guise of economic development.

The answer to the massive land and water degradation problems we are faced with lies fairly and squarely in the hands of individuals. Ordinary people like you and me. Whether we live on the land, in a country town or in a city, none of us can escape its consequences. It affects us all in one way or another.

We must be vigilant and be aware that there is no instant panacea for our past mistakes. The care and rehabilitation of our land and its resources requires an ongoing commitment. If we neglect our responsibilities then our soil will continue to be lost or rendered unproductive, our rivers and waterways will die and the plants and animals that depend on them will slide down the path to oblivion. Once lost, a plant or animal can never be regained. After all, extinction has a certain finality about it.

# She-Oaks

*Casuarina* spp.

*Allocasuarina* spp.

'Witjweri' is the Aboriginal name given to the sound that the wind makes through the 'leaves' of she-oaks. Most of us would have heard this haunting, wailing sound because these trees occur all over Australia from the coast to the driest parts of our deserts.

There are dozens of different kinds of she-oaks. Some are shrubs while others grow into fairly large trees. They are all virtually leafless. Their long, cylindrical, pendulous 'leaves' are really small branches which behave like true leaves.

It's not certain how the word 'she' got its origin. Perhaps it is because of the occurrence of female trees in some species but maybe the name derives from the sound 'shee'—the sound of the wind in the trees. Yet another explanation is that it was the early settlers' way of indicating the wood's inferiority compared to true oaks.

The largest of the she-oaks grow to thirty-five metres, or about 100 feet high. These, the river she-oaks, occur in narrow belts along creeks and rivers in eastern Australia, from southern New South Wales to northern Queensland and the Territory. Like all she-oaks it has a number of common names. Queenslanders may know it as creek oak.

The timber of this tree was once used for roofing shingles and bullock yokes. It, along with all other she-oaks, makes excellent firewood, burning extremely hot. The river she-oak is completely protected in New South Wales, mainly because of its value in protecting creek and river banks from erosion.

The desert she-oak of central Australia thrives in areas receiving as little as 100mm or 4 inches of rain a year. This makes it one of our most important and useful trees for planting in arid climates. Aborigines valued these trees because their often hollow trunks provided valuable water reservoirs.

Others, such as the swamp she-oak of the eastern coast and the Western Australian swamp she-oak, can tolerate very salty conditions. These have potential for planting in areas where many other trees cannot grow.

She-oaks are highly adaptable and have been planted in many overseas countries. They are used for wind breaks, soil conservation, shade, drought, fodder, ornamental purposes and firewood production. So highly are they regarded in India that some of the better-off landholders have planted she-oaks as a dowry for their daughters.

She-oaks once belonged to one genus, *Casuarina*. However taxonomists got to them and split them into *Casuarina* and *Allocasuarina*. Now there are six kinds of *Casuarina* and fifty-nine kinds of *Allocasuarina* in Australia. All up, they have well over 100 common names.

All are not called she-oaks. In fact all don't have oak in their common name. Some of their names are pronounced the same but spelt differently. Bull oak, for example, is also spelt buloke. Sometimes bull oak is two words, sometimes it is hyphenated, sometimes it is written as one word. Unlike belah, the foliage of bull oak is not normally eaten by stock. Belah, by the way, is sometimes called bull oak. There is even a rainforest tree that grows near Townsville that's called bull oak. We have a small bull oak that is confined to Kangaroo Island and the nearby mainland while the black she-oak of the eastern coast is also called bull oak. Confusion reigns.

# Turpentine

## *Syncarpia glomulifera*

When you catch a ferry from a wharf or are fishing from your favourite pier or jetty, chances are that the timber used in its construction will be turpentine, at least along our eastern seaboard anyway.

Of all Australia's timbers, turpentine is the most resistant to attack by marine borers, especially if the resinous bark is left intact. For this reason it is used extensively for building all sorts of structures which are in contact with sea water. These include everything from wharfs and jetties to channel markers and even underwater boat planking.

Turpentine's other claim to fame is that it is one of the world's most resistant timbers to damage by fire. It is very hard to ignite and is a dead loss as far as firewood is concerned.

Obviously, its common name is not very apt. The tree doesn't burn easily nor does it smell like the turpentine that is used when painting. True turpentine is obtained from certain pine trees in the northern hemisphere.

Turpentine grows to a large tree with thick, fibrous, stringy bark. It has a dense crown and the leaves are dark green with a much paler undersurface. Although it is not a eucalypt, it is closely related and is in the same family. Its natural occurrence is confined to coastal and near-coastal areas and extends from Batemans Bay in southern New South Wales to well up into Queensland.

Just across the road from the house that I grew up in there was a grove of a dozen or so fairly large turpentine trees. The paddock in which they grew wasn't particularly large and the trees were its focal point. They provided a good hide-out for us kids, somewhere we could congregate after school or during weekends, where we must have shot ourselves hundreds and hundreds of times when dressed up as Cowboys or Indians.

And get dressed up we did! We wore the whole regalia, everything from double holstered six guns, hats, sheriff badges and Lone Ranger masks if you were a Cowboy, or long feathered head-dresses and war painted faces, arms and chests if it was your turn to be an Indian. You were supposed to fall over if shot. If you didn't you weren't playing fair. Inevitably the cowboys always seemed to win. The bows and arrows of the Indians were obviously no match for the guns and caps of the Cowboys.

Younger brothers were a nuisance. They didn't seem to understand the intricacies of how to play properly. If you were waiting in ambush they would give you away and you would get shot or an arrow in your back.

Girls, of course, were a definite no no. If one dared to venture too close to the action, she would be shot by the Cowboys *and* the Indians. She wasn't expected to fall over though, just merely go home.

Our secret hide-out amongst the turpentines and the tall kangaroo grass that surrounded it has now given way to three bedroom brick veneers surrounded by manicured lawns and paling fences. The children that live there don't play Cowboys and Indians; they most likely dress up as turtles.

# Rosewood

*Alectryon oleifolius* (inland)

*Dysoxylum fraserianum* (rainforest)

Rosewood is a small rounded tree with greyish-green leaves and grows in the dry country from Carnarvon to Rockhampton. To look at, it resembles an olive tree, and is very common especially on limestone soils. The trees are nearly always browsed by everything from sheep to cattle and goats. The dense crown provides good shade and birds find the thick foliage ideal for nesting.

Rosewood suckers freely from its roots but although it produces stacks of glossy black seeds I have never seen a seedling growing naturally.

As we know, common names of trees can be very confusing. There are some sixteen common names applied to this tree. To South Australians, it's bullock bush, in the West it's known as minga. In the Riverina, the locals refer to it as applebush.

To add even more confusion, one of our tallest rainforest trees is also known as rosewood. This tree can grow up to 160 feet or 50 metres high and is found in the rainforests of the eastern coast from Wyong in New South Wales to just over the border into Queensland.

It is a valuable timber tree and back when supplies were plentiful it was used extensively in the furniture trade. The common name of rosewood derives from the pleasant rose-like perfume of its wood.

The two rosewoods, the one found in the dry inland areas and the other, the large rainforest tree, are in no way related. Nor, obviously, are the environments in which they live.

The inland areas of Australia are frequently swept by fires and the trees which grow there are able to regenerate in various ways after such events. Not so in the case of rainforest trees. Even with the slightest contact, fire will kill them.

This is one of the reasons that clearing rainforests is relatively easy. The trees do not have the ability to regrow by shooting from their trunk, their branches or suckering from their roots.

There are thousands of small patches of intact rainforest that have escaped the axe and the bulldozer. The preservation of these areas is a noble goal. However, great care should be taken that they *do* remain intact. Any surrounding trees on the perimeter should be left and of course fire must be avoided at all costs.

# Snow Gums

*Eucalyptus pauciflora*
*Eucalyptus niphophila*

With the onset of winter and snowfalls imminent in the high country, the first trees that will be clothed in snow are the snow gums. These are the well known trees of the Thredbo and Falls Creek skiing set and are easily recognised by the small, yellow, circular patch of snow behind most trees.

Snow gums are just one of the 600 or so species of *Eucalyptus* and they occur mainly on the mountainous areas of New South Wales, Victoria and Tasmania but extend into parts of South Australia and even Queensland. At Kosciusko they cease at an altitude of about 1800 metres and are therefore the 'highest' trees in Australia. Occasionally they are also found at lower altitudes, almost to sea level in parts of Tassie and near Bega in New South Wales and Mt Gambier in South Australia.

At high altitudes, especially where exposed to the extremes of windy and cold conditions, they grow to only a small twisted tree, somewhat resembling a large bonsai. It is these forms that have been the focus of many a photographer. The shape of the tree and the range of the beautiful whites, greens, yellows, greys, blues and reds of the bark make snow gums a popular subject.

It's not just the tree itself that is so spectacular but it's the environment in which it lives that makes it so special. Stunted snow gums, grey rocky outcrops, spongy green snowgrass with masses of wildflowers in spring, crystal clear cold streams, and crisp invigorating mountain air provide the ingredients for this unique part of Australia.

In winter, deep snowdrifts and the steely grey rocks provide an almost monochromatic background for the snow gums in this harsh environment.

When snow gums are burnt they behave similarly to the mallees. If the tops are killed regeneration is achieved by numerous suckers which arise from the underground rootstock. These grow rapidly at first and then thin out as some become dominant and grow to form a multi-stemmed tree. Pretty well all the dense snow gums you see in Kosciusko National Park and on the Bogong High Plains in Victoria are a legacy of past bushfires.

The whole question of fire in the high country poses a management dilemma. Since the abolition of grazing in the Kosciusko National Park there has been a build-up of vegetation, especially shrubs. It is these that provide the fuel necessary to carry a fire. When the country was being grazed the stockmen would burn small patches in the autumn to encourage fresh growth for their stock the following spring. These fires also kept a check on the shrubs.

In many places on the Bogong High Plains in Victoria shrubs are also increasing, especially where cattle have not been grazed for a number of years. The debate on the summer grazing of cattle on the High Plains is an emotive one and is too often coloured by subjective and value judgements. However, summer grazing by cattle and the associated folklore is an integral feature of Australia's heritage and for this reason many believe it should be allowed to continue.

In the early days cattlemen used snow gum to construct their huts in the high country. Today, many of these huts are still standing and are used by bushwalkers and lost skiers as well as by cattlemen when mustering in autumn before the snow sets in. Most of them are in good condition and have changed little except where a galvanised roof has replaced the original wooden shingles.

# Mountain Ash

*Eucalyptus regnans*

The Cornthwaite Tree, the King of the Cumberland, the Furmston Tree and the Ada Tree are (or were) all mountain ash, they are all in Victoria and have been variously claimed to be the tallest tree on the Australian mainland.

These giant eucalypts, the mountain ash, are found only in Victoria and Tasmania. The Maydena Tree in Tassie holds the current record for the tallest standing tree in Australia at the present time. It is a little over 98 metres or 320 feet high. The Ada Tree is about 70 metres or 276 feet high and is Victoria's tallest.

The award for the tallest tree on Earth goes to a redwood in California but mountain ash are the tallest hardwood and the tallest flowering plants on our planet.

Mountain ash is one of our major timber trees and in Victoria is confined to the cool mountains in the eastern half of the State as well as Mt. Macedon near Melbourne and the Otway Ranges.

Rather strangely they are not particularly long-lived: three to four hundred years seems to be about their maximum life-span. That's nothing when compared to some American trees which have lived for three to four thousand years.

Unlike most eucalypts, mountain ash are easily killed by fire. Regeneration occurs entirely from seed. Following the passage of a bushfire, seed is released and rains down onto the fertile ash bed of the forest floor and, given the right conditions, they germinate and begin to grow rapidly skywards.

Following the devastating bushfires of 1939 in Victoria, hundreds of square miles of dense, even-aged stands of the tree developed. It is quick growing and is regarded as one of the best of the eucalypts for the pulp mills and paper industry. Large quantities are also used for housing construction, furniture and plywood. In the early days the forests were first exploited for palings and shingles as the timber splits easily and is easy to work.

Forests of mountain ash, or any of our other tall eucalypts for that matter, are a majestic sight, sometimes even eerie. I recall walking through a forest near Marysville one foggy winter's morning a couple of years ago. Looking up, all I could see were the huge straight trunks of the trees disappearing into the mist. There was not the slightest breath of wind and the only sound was the constant dripping of water from the leaves and branches hidden by the mist way above.

# Mulga

*Acacia aneura*

If any one tree typifies the vast, dry inland it would have to be mulga. It occurs right across Australia from central New South Wales to the Indian Ocean and from Spencers Gulf to within a couple of hundred kilometres of Darwin. Plant communities dominated by mulga account for about one and a half million square kilometres.

Mulga is one of the more than 700 or so kinds of *Acacia* which are found in Australia. The size and shape of mulgas varies immensely—it can occur as a tree with a single straight trunk or as a multi-stemmed shrub.

Its 'leaves' are also extremely variable and range from needle-like to quite flat and long and it can flower at almost any time of the year depending on favourable rains. The flowers are not as spectacular as many of our other acacias but the attractive nature of the tree is due to its distinctive silvery-grey foliage.

Mulga is a good example of how a relatively large and long-lived plant copes with the extremes of heat and drought. Unlike the eucalypts and most other acacias, its foliage is arranged so that it points upward avoiding the direct rays of the sun. In drought times it stops growing, drops many of its leaves and is able to survive without any water at all. When rain comes again the drops of water are directed down the branches that slant upwards from the main trunk. In this way most of the precious water is channelled down the stem and enters the soil where it can be drawn on by the roots. This is one of its secrets for survival in the arid interior of Australia where it flourishes in areas that receive as little as five inches (200mm) of rain a year.

Mulga is undoubtedly our most important fodder tree, not because it is particularly nutritious to stock but because it is so widespread, common and palatable. In times of drought when grass and other feed is scarce, branches are cut to provide food for starving sheep. In the old days this was done by axe but nowadays the chainsaw and even bulldozers and tractors have taken over.

During the great drought at the turn of the century, and even during subsequent ones, large sheep stations would employ gangs of fifty men full-time cutting mulga in order to keep their sheep alive.

Over the years the tree has provided the posts for a myriad miles of fencing and has fuelled the fires of countless homesteads and stock camps.

Polished mulga wood is used extensively in the manufacture of various ornamental articles. We all would have seen these items in souvenir shops—everything from pen and ink stands to book-ends.

That smelly dishmop (although not much in vogue these days) may be banished from your kitchen forever by substituting a small branch of mulga which has had the end bashed until it turns to fibre—guaranteed not to stink and instantly replaceable for nix, as long as you have a mulga tree handy.

The Aborigines, of course, used mulga extensively. It was used to make boomerangs, spears, digging sticks, clubs and shields. In fact, the word 'mulga' comes from an Aboriginal word for a long narrow shield made from the tree.

# Quandong

*Santalum acuminatum*

Without a doubt one of our most attractive small native trees would have to be the quandongs. During spring and early summer they bear masses of bright red fruit up to about an inch in diameter which contrast against the grey-green foliage and are fairly easily spotted.

The quandong is found in all the mainland states and thrives in the hot dry inland regions. Like other members of its family it is partially parasitic on the roots of other plants. The famed sandalwood of South Australia and Western Australia, which is exported to Asian countries to make joss sticks, belongs to the same genus.

Amongst country people the quandong is probably the best known bush tucker. The fruit is highly nutritious and contains about twice the amount of vitamin C as oranges. Quandongs can be eaten raw but are rather tart. They are best when cooked and used in pies, jams and jellies. In areas where the trees are still found, housewives take great pride in serving their guests quandong pie for sweets or as a spread on toast for breakfast.

It's not only the fleshy part of the fruit that can be eaten. Within the stone there is an oily seed but its taste is not all that great. It is marginally better when lightly roasted.

The bright red fruits are a favourite diet of emus and wherever there are quandongs in fruit there are bound to be emus about. The spotted bower bird collects the fruit to adorn his bower which is invariably constructed under the low hanging branches of a wilga. Both these birds, and undoubtedly others, play a major role in dispersing the seed.

Those of us who still have an old set of Chinese checkers hidden away somewhere will find that the coloured marbles are, in fact, the pitted stones of the quandong. In the past the stones have also been used for making necklaces.

Quandongs can be successfully grown from seed but when the seedling is a couple of inches high a host plant has to be provided so that the young seedling can parasitise its roots. Commonly, kikuyu or lucerne is used as the host plant but others will do the trick just as well.

Grevillea

Dillon Bush

Berrigan

Biddy Bush

Yarran

Snow Gum

Beefwood

Buloke

Saltbush

Mallee

Mallee regrowth after fire

River Red Gum

Cooba

Rosewoods

Peppertrees

Quandong

Gidgee

Mulga

Golden-top Wattle

Mitchell Grass

Coolibah

Corkwood (Hakea)

Needlewood (Hakea)

Kurrajongs

Wilga

Athel Trees

Christmas Bush (NSW)

Tasmanian Blue Gum

Banksia

Mistletoe

Red Cedar

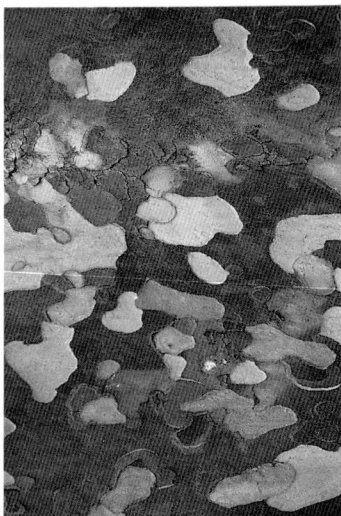

Plane Tree bark

Plane Tree

Wild Orange—browsed by goats

Acacia

Mangroves

White Cypress Pine

White Cypress Pine —pollen laden

# Rabbits—the Biological Chainsaws

For the first half of this century generations of country people never saw a young cypress pine, kurrajong or mulga.

Millions and millions of rabbits ate any seedlings that came up. Even large, established trees didn't escape. They ate the bark off mature kurrajongs and even climbed and ate the leaves off some trees. Pastures degenerated and the outback became a huge dustbowl.

The first rabbits to arrive in Australia came with the First Fleet but it wasn't until they were released near Geelong in 1859 that they really got a foothold and began their march across the country. They reached Queensland in the late 1880s and by 1907 had arrived on the shores of the Indian Ocean in Western Australia. Nowadays they inhabit every corner of our country except for the far north.

It seems that rabbits had help in their colonisation of Australia. Bags and crates of rabbits were transported by river boats and rail. However, it was soon realised that rabbits posed a real threat to the farming and pastoral industries.

Farmers and graziers employed thousands of men in a vain attempt to halt their progress. The most common method of controlling their numbers in the early days was by poisoning waterholes. Pit traps were dug, warrens were fumigated and ripped and poison baits laid out. Rabbit-proof fences only temporarily slowed their progress. Cats were released and goannas were declared an enemy of the rabbit and were protected. Millions of Lane's Ace traps were manufactured and sold. All in vain.

However, the tide finally turned against the rabbit with the success of myxomatosis in the early 1950s.

Trees sprang up again, cypress pines in the Pilliga forest in New South Wales came up *en masse*. Seedlings of mulgas and scores of other trees and shrubs of the inland appeared once again.

Over the years rabbits have fed countless families during the lean times and have provided employment for thousands of men and pocket money for just as many children. The rabbit trade still remains an important industry. Without the humble rabbit, we wouldn't have our Akubras. Each hat requires the fur of sixteen to eighteen rabbits and, with 700 dozen hats made every week, that means a hell of a lot of rabbits.

# Railways and Cemeteries

What do railways and cemeteries have in common?

Cynics might say that they either contain, or are, relics of the past but the answer is that they provide important refuges for many of our native plants.

Railway lines are usually fenced off from adjacent paddocks or roads. Such areas have been left essentially undisturbed for well over 100 years. The same applies to cemeteries, especially the neglected corners of those found in small country towns.

If you want to find out what kind of plants originally grew in your locality then a stroll beside the railway line or through your local cemetery can often give a clue.

Most of the longer-lived plants growing beside trainlines are well adapted to fire because the land was regularly burnt as a safeguard against bushfires setting fire to the sleepers. Burning off was also important in the days of the steam locos when the likelihood of fire from the red-hot brake pads of trains going down a steep grade was ever-present. It used to be said that many bushfires were started in this way by trains descending the Blue Mountains in New South Wales.

A good example of a native plant that was once more widespread, and which can now only be found in railway reserves and cemeteries in many parts of Australia, is kangaroo grass. It has survived in these places because it is well adapted to fire and has been protected from heavy grazing.

Railway cuttings through solid rock, like the ones around the Sydney region, provide an ideal habitat for many shade-loving plants, especially ferns. They cling tenaciously to small crevices in the rocky walls and thrive in this seemingly hostile environment.

Of course it's not only native plants that grow and prosper along trainlines or in cemeteries. Myriads of weeds find such places to their liking as well.

The massed display of yellow *Calliopsis* along railway embankments is a familiar sight to many people. To some, this daisy-like flower brings great delight, but to others it is a scourge, which should be stopped in its tracks and not allowed to spread any further. I recall my biology teacher at school spending weekends pulling out these plants in a vain attempt to arrest their spread.

It was futile. The story goes that *Calliopsis* seeds were deliberately thrown out of train windows. They literally rode the rails and the plant's successful invasion was assured.

It seems inevitable that the demise of miles and miles of our railways right across Australia will lead to the local extinction of numerous native plants. Once the trains stop running and the fences are taken down or fall into a state of disrepair, the land will be grazed or used for some other purpose. The plants which depended on these areas will go the same way as our trains—on the downward track to extinction.

# Mitchell Grass

*Astrebla* spp.

The decline or absence of trees over many parts of Australia has received a great deal of publicity and is a genuine cause of concern among people from numerous walks of life. However, not all parts of Australia are, or ever were, dominated by trees.

One such area is the 300 000 square kilometres-plus of Mitchell grasslands that stretch in a great arc from the Kimberley in Western Australia, across the Territory, through Queensland and into northern New South Wales. It is the lack of trees that typifies these grasslands, especially on the Barkly Tablelands in the Northern Territory and around Longreach, Winton and Julia Creek in Queensland.

The only trees in these parts are to be found along the watercourses where various gums and acacias grow, the sole providers of shade for the sheep and cattle that graze these lands.

Mitchell grass owes its name to the explorer-cum-surveyor Sir Thomas Mitchell who collected the first specimens from near Bourke in 1835, Condobolin in 1836 and in Queensland in 1846.

Mitchell grass is a tussock-forming perennial grass. Individual plants can live in excess of twenty years. There are four kinds—curly, barley, bull and weeping or hoop. They all grow on heavy, cracking clay soils that after rain become a huge gluepot to the unwary. Even the initiated local dreads sliding off a formed track and becoming bogged up to the axles. The only way to extricate a vehicle in this predicament is to wait until the ground dries—and this can take many days sometimes.

The Mitchell grass country supports large numbers of sheep in New South Wales and Queensland and cattle in the Territory and Western Australia. It is regarded as 'good' grazing country, especially after rains when the fertile soils bring forth a smorgasbord of succulent, mouth-watering annual plants that stock thrive, fatten and breed upon. These grasses can survive long periods of drought. Their massive, deep underground parts remain in a kind of hibernation ready to commence growth once sufficient rain comes. This makes them one of our most valued perennial grasses.

Mitchell grass country is relatively resistant to the ravages of our domestic stock. The grass is long-lived and the soils and flat landscapes it grows upon do not erode easily. The plants themselves are not particularly attractive to stock but their value comes in times when the rains don't fall. They provide a kind of drought reserve in the same way as do saltbush and mulga in other parts of Australia.

Individual plants can grow up to one or one and a half metres high, bull Mitchell being the tallest. In some years they seed prolifically but it's only once every ten to twenty years that large numbers of seedlings are produced and survive. This has important repercussions for the continued survival and replacement of these remarkable grasses.

To me, the vast rolling downs of Mitchell grass country means being able to see the curvature of the earth; it means seeing a windmill or the outline of a turkey nest tank on the horizon. It means a lush green sea of waving grass after rain and it means a hot shimmering yellow endlessness during summer.

There are some unforgettable memories that I associate with the treeless expanses of this country. The first is being besieged by thousands upon thousands of native plague rats when camped out one night, sitting by the campfire. They came in their hordes and ate anything they could get their teeth into. I vividly remember them gnawing at my boots while I was drinking a Bundy and attempting to cook tea on the campfire.

A year or so later I was caught in an early monsoonal rainstorm in north western Queensland and as the cattle hoof prints were filled and the country became awash with water, small fish suddenly appeared swimming in their small, private and very temporary waterholes. The following day their domain had dried and evaporated and their only legacy was the eggs they had left behind waiting for the right conditions to begin the life cyle all over again.

I have never seen it rain cats and dogs but I have seen it rain fish!

# Mangroves

The Hunter River at Maitland was once the site of a thriving soap-making industry. In the 1840s hundreds of acres of mangroves were cut down. The trunks, stems and leaves were dragged across the mud flats and stacked out of reach of the tide. The piles would be lit and burnt to a fine white ash. The ash was called 'barilla', rich in the essential ingredients for the manufacture of soap.

Mangrove cutting was not confined to the Maitland area. The practice occurred all along the east coast from Queensland to Victoria. In Sydney, mangrove cutting began around 1810 and reached a peak in the 1840s. The discovery of how to chemically convert common salt to soda spelt the doom of the barilla industry. Mangroves obtained a reprieve.

To the majority of people mangroves and the thick black ooze in which they grow are definitely places to be avoided. Lets face it, crocodiles, myriads of mossies and a host of other nasties make their home there.

This perceived hostile nature of the mangrove environment has undoubtedly been responsible for much of its demise. In the eyes of some they are uninviting, useless wastelands and as such are targeted for 'development'. In their place we now have golf courses, marinas and five-star foreign-owned tourist resorts.

However, without a doubt the greatest value of mangroves and their environment is that they provide a nursery for the marine food chain. Mangroves are essential to the prawn fishermen of the Gulf as they are essential for the continued well-being and existence of much of our fishing industry along the coast. As such they should be preserved.

Mangroves are found in all States except Tasmania. They are shrubs or small trees which grow in the intertidal zone of the coastline and estuaries. They favour the northern regions and gradually peter out towards the south. There is only one kind in the southern parts of Australia, the grey or white mangrove.

This species is one of the largest and grows up to eight metres high. Seedlings of this mangrove actually develop while still attached to the parent tree. When they are a couple of inches long they drop into the mud below and immediately grow roots. So quick is this process that before the tide comes in the young plant has a good hold and can't be washed away.,

A truly remarkable tree, completely adapted to surviving in its harsh, salty environment.

# Mistletoe

There are many examples in the natural world of interesting associations between different organisms. Sometimes these are beneficial to both but often they only benefit one.

A common, one-sided alliance in Australia exists between mistletoe, its host plant and the mistletoe bird. It is one-sided because while the mistletoe plant and the mistletoe bird derive a kind of mutual benefit from each other, the host tree misses out.

Mistletoe can be found from Melbourne to Melville Island and from Maroochydore to Manjimup. Strangely, it is absent from Tasmania.

While the practice of kissing under mistletoe has never really caught on in Australia, mistletoe has been associated overseas with myth and magic for many centuries. In European countries it was cut from trees with great ritual and ceremony and was wonderful for warding off witches, worrying the hell out of evil spirits as well as being widely used in various medicinal concoctions.

Mistletoe is a parasitic plant that grows on the branches of other trees. Actually, it is only partly parasitic because although it gets water and some nutrients from its host, its green leaves manufacture its own supply of food by capturing the sun's rays.

Mistletoes vary in leaf shape and colour as well as in flower colour. One of the particularly noticeable things when you look at mistletoe is that the leaves tend to resemble the foliage of the tree that it's growing on. Needle-leaf mistletoe has long, thin cylindrical leaves just like those of its host plant, the she-oak. On the other hand, the common box mistletoe has flat leaves the same size and shape as the eucalypt it grows upon.

Why do mistletoes bother to camouflage themselves in this way? It could be that they rate high in the culinary delights of possums and that the chance of being eaten is diminished if the mistletoe takes on a look-alike appearance of its host tree.

Mistletoes provide a veritable smorgasbord of food for a large range of animals. Caterpillars of numerous butterflies feed on the leaves and honeyeaters are attracted by brightly coloured, nectar-rich flowers. The most important bird, though, is the mistletoe bird which occurs wherever the plant is found. This beautiful small bird eagerly seeks out the ripe, fleshy, sticky fruit and spreads the undigested seed to another tree where it can germinate and grow.

Often mistletoe may cause the end of the branch that it is living on to die and occasionally a tree with too many free-loaders on it will succumb with the result that the entire tree will turn its toes up and perish.

# Mallee

## Eucalyptus spp.

Some of the most interesting kinds of eucalypts occurring over vast areas of Australia are the mallees. The word mallee came from the Aborigines who used the term 'mali' to describe the water mallee whose lateral roots provided a source of drinking water.

The use of the term by Europeans commenced in the middle of last century and today it is used to describe the 300 000 square kilometres of country stretching across southern Australia from New South Wales to Western Australia which is dominated by these small multi-stemmed *Eucalyptus* trees.

There are at least 100 species of mallee although not all are confined to the 'mallee country'. For example in parts of south eastern Queensland and on the Blue Mountains west of Sydney some mallees find the poor rocky soils to their liking.

Heights of mallees range from about one to ten metres and one plant can have a dozen or more stems. Mallees with several thin stems are referred to as 'whipstick' mallee whereas those with only a few thick stems are sometimes termed 'bull' mallee. Whipstick mallee stems make really beaut tomato stakes.

Mallee stems arise from a swollen underground rootstock called a lignotuber. These lignotubers can grow exceedingly large and can commonly weigh up to a tonne or more and may measure well over one metre across. Their lifespan is measured in hundreds of years which makes them amongst the longest lived of the eucalypts.

Mallee lignotubers are highly sought after as firewood and bring big money in places such as Melbourne.

Thousands upon thousands of acres of mallee have been cleared to make way for wheat crops, especially in north western Victoria, south western New South Wales and South Australia. The fragile nature of the sandy mallee soils led to massive problems of sand drift and erosion and stories abound of mallee farmers going broke, especially during the post-war periods when governments introduced soldier settler schemes. Blocks of 640 acres, or one square mile, were laboriously cleared and sown only to see the crop wither and die during times of drought. What topsoil there was, was blown away, with fences, roads and waterholes disappearing under the moving soil.

Although there remain serious erosion problems, and more recently problems of salinity, clearing in this marginal cropping country requires strips of untouched mallee to be left so that the risk of further erosion is minimised.

Clearing mallee country also has repercussions for the unique malleefowl—the bird that builds its own incubator to hatch its eggs. Loss of its habitat has probably reduced the number of these remarkable birds. Continued clearing, together with predation by foxes and feral cats, may well place the malleefowl at risk.

The leaves of certain kinds of mallee are used for the production of Eucalyptus oil. Natural stands of blue mallee (*Eucalyptus polybractea*) near Bendigo in Victoria and West Wyalong in New South Wales have been harvested for many years. Commercial production began in 1907 and in the 1920s up to fifty men were employed in the West Wyalong district to cut and distil the oil from the mallee leaves. Nowadays, Eucalyptus oil is still produced but not in the quantitites it was once. It may be a surprise to learn that China, South Africa, Portugal, Spain and Brazil all export more Eucalyptus oil than we do!

# Kurrajong

## Brachychiton populneum

One of the most attractive trees in *Wild and Free* is the kurrajong. There are a number of different types occurring throughout Australia. The common one in New South Wales and Queensland and the only one that is found in Victoria is a medium-sized tree which can grow up to twenty metres. It has a relatively short, thick, grey trunk with a dense rounded canopy of bright green leaves which stands out against the other trees of more sombre colours. The leaves are extremely variable: even on one tree there can be broad and poplar-like leaves while others are angular and highly divided.

Kurrajongs occur as scattered individuals and are often left as the sole remaining tree in cleared paddocks in the wheat and sheep belt. Beautiful old kurrajongs also occur on top of numerous rocky hills in the interior of New South Wales and their inscribed and initialled trunks bear testimony to those who have made the ascent.

They are unsurpassed as shade trees and during drought periods when natural pastures are scarce they can be lopped to provide excellent stock fodder. The trees are drought-resistant and readily reshoot even after fairly severe lopping. Kurrajongs are commonly planted along streets and in parks of country towns, in sheepyards and homestead gardens. They are easy to raise from seed and young plants can successfully be transplanted.

Some are evergreen, some semi-deciduous but the red-flowering kurrajong of the Northern Territory is completely deciduous in the dry season, and its bright red flowers have been adopted as the floral emblem of Darwin. Perhaps the most spectacular one is the Illawarra flame which produces masses of red bell shaped flowers.

Beside being excellent shade, fodder and ornamental trees they provided a source of food and water for Aborigines and explorers. The cooked swollen roots of young plants were a popular food item with the Aborigines. When ripe, the large boat-shaped pods or fruit contain numerous yellow seeds, about the size of a pea, which may be eaten raw or roasted. They can also be used as a substitute for coffee after they are lightly roasted, ground and then boiled. Indeed, the seeds actually contain caffeine. The explorer Leichhardt recorded that the seeds 'produced a good beverage with an agreeable flavour'. Kurrajongs are one of the better water trees, the cut roots can yield large amounts of good clean water.

Unfortunately it is rare to find a young kurrajong growing naturally except in areas which are protected from grazing. Large, very old trees are common in cleared paddocks and grazing lands, but unless fenced-off areas are set aside, seedlings won't be able to establish, and their population will slowly decline and kurrajongs will cease to exist in their natural environment.

# Kalgoorlie

One of the things that has always fascinated people is the rich flora of Western Australia. Not only is it renowned for the spectacular wildflower displays in spring but in Western Australia there are hundreds and hundreds of plants which occur nowhere else in Australia. This is particularly the case in the south west of the State. The region around Kalgoorlie is no exception.

The reasons for this are complex but the isolation from eastern Australia caused by the great deserts and the Nullarbor Plain have obviously played an important role.

Kalgoorlie is of course famous for its gold mines and the notoriety that such a frontier town attracted, especially in its early days. The 'Golden Mile' between Kalgoorlie and the adjacent town of Boulder has undoubtedly brought all sorts of wealth and pleasures to countless prospectors.

Kalgoorlie lies close to the edge of the desert and only 160 miles from the Nullarbor. It receives less than ten inches of rain a year and has to pipe its water from the ranges a couple of hundred miles nearer Perth.

However, despite the very low rainfall, Kalgoorlie's streets, parks and gardens support an astonishing number of trees which thrive in the hot, dry climate.

The key to the successful greening of Kalgoorlie has been that most of the trees that have been planted are native to the area.

Perhaps you would expect that in such an inhospitable climate the native plants would be plants like saltbushes and the ubiquitous mulgas. Although these do occur, there are other plants that find the harsh conditions to their liking. Some of the most noteworthy are gums. The salmon gum is one of these and is one of our most remarkable eucalypts because it can grow up to 100 feet (30 metres) or so in country that receives less than ten inches of rain. It gets its common name from the colour of its bark which turns salmon pink at certain times of the year.

Not all the local trees grow this tall of course but others are outstanding for other reasons. Another eucalypt, the coral or Coolgardie gum is spectacular because of its masses of pink blossoms. Like many other Western Australian eucalypts it has been widely planted throughout the country and graces many large inland towns and cities.

# Hakea

*Hakea* spp.

Hakeas are a group of around 140 or so species which occur just about everywhere in Australia except for rainforests. They are closely related to the grevilleas, banksias and waratahs and vary from small shrubs to trees up to ten metres high. In their natural habitat they are more often than not straggly and untidy looking plants and although some have broad, leathery leaves, many have prickly needle-shaped leaves and for this reason don't rate too highly in the popularity stakes amongst all but the most dedicated native gardeners. On the plus side they display masses of large flowers ranging through reds, oranges, yellows to creams and whites. They have been unfairly neglected as a garden plant and there are plenty to choose from if you don't want prickly types.

Small birds, of course, find that the prickly hakeas are an ideal safe nesting site. Feral cats and even your pet moggy will find things very unpleasant if they attempt to raid a nest that has been built amongst the spiky leaves.

The family of plants to which *Hakea* belongs, the Proteaceae, are renowned for attracting nectar-feeding insects and birds. Another plus for your garden.

Like most native plants *Hakea* has evolved in the presence of fire and has developed ways of surviving fire. Some species have lignotubers which send up new stems after being burnt. Most hakeas retain their seeds in woody capsules until the fire has long passed and only then do they release their seeds to germinate as soon as it rains. In places where fire occurs every few years, some hakeas have formed impenetrable thickets.

Needlewood (*Hakea leucoptera*) is a fairly common shrub

or small tree which is found in the drier areas of all mainland states. As its name suggests there is no prize for guessing what kind of leaves it has. Another of its common names is water tree, derived because Aborigines used it to obtain drinking water when times were tough. A piece of root, a couple of metres long, was held with one end over a fire and the other above a container to catch the water dripping out.

The timber from needlewood is very hard and has been used for making small turnery articles. In 1895 The Australian Needlewood Pipe Company was established in Sydney to produce tobacco pipes from its roots. The quality of these pipes was supposed to be superior to the English briar pipes but connoisseurs apparently thought otherwise. The company soon folded.

Hakeas were introduced into the United Kingdom as early as 1790 and today some of the non-prickly ones are popular in many overseas countries. However, in parts of fire-prone South Africa some hakeas have become weeds because of their ability to come up following fire.

# Gidgee

## Acacia cambagei

Most of the decorative wattles grown in gardens are renowned for their short life spans. However this is not a trait of all acacias. There are many that live for long periods of time. One such *Acacia* is gidgee.

Gidgee occurs in the dry areas of New South Wales, Queensland, South Australia and the Northern Territory and quite often grows in thick stands containing very few other kinds of trees or shrubs. In these situations the ground is usually devoid of anything much in the way of pasture except for the odd spiny copperburrs. Much of this sort of country has been cleared to make way for more productive pastures.

Some trees can be fairly large by *Acacia* standards with trunk diameters approaching 60 cm or 2 ft. Considering gidgee is very slow growing such trees must be very old. They may well have been young trees when Captain Cook sailed into Botany Bay.

Gidgee has a number of claims to fame. It is renowned for the rather sickly, foetid smell its leaves give off, particularly after a shower of rain. To many people, especially those not accustomed to it, the aroma is not to their liking but after a couple of days in gidgee country it becomes less of a problem.

Strainer posts made from the trunk are about the best you can get; they last for years and stand up well to the eating habits of white ants. The wood is extremely hard and cutting it with a chainsaw really takes the edge off things. However, if it is used for firewood, the effort is worthwhile, because it burns with an intense heat leaving a fine white ash.

Gidgees are rather dark, solemn looking trees and their pale yellow blossoms aren't all that spectacular. They make good shade trees for sheep and their qualities as fence posts make them a valuable asset on pastoral properties.

Gidgee is one of those trees that feature in bush stories, songs and folklore. They have become synonomous with everything from galahs to gidgee-itch, the latter being an allergic skin reaction that affects some people.

When country and western singer Rex Dallas was sitting by a fire of gidgee on the banks of the Murrumbidgee he must have carted the wood a long way—gidgee doesn't occur that far south.

# Firewood

As much as I have a great affection for any tree, I can't deny there is a special magic about an open fireplace in a home. Keeping up the supply of wood, however, can be quite an experience. It's amazing how I suddenly have to go and get the winter's quota of firewood. The catalyst for this is when the rest of the family produce blankets to wrap around themselves to watch the TV news at night. 'Gee, it would be nice to have the fire on tonight', comes the chorus.

Round here in the southern Riverina, they reckon that box is the best wood to burn. Redgum or, more accurately, river red gum is supposed to be inferior—it doesn't burn away as well, it soots up the chimney and doesn't give out as much heat. I really don't find much difference. The most important thing to remember is to make sure that the wood is well dried—that is, it's been dead for a minimum of ten years.

At least cutting redgum is infinitely easier and kinder on a chainsaw. You haven't got to sharpen or replace the chain nearly as often. Box is a much harder wood.

It's good when you come across a fallen tree with all its branches about waist high and can work your way along each one. I found such a tree a few weeks back. It was an old box that had fallen many years ago and had stacks of good wood in it. I began by attacking a rather large hollow branch, slicing through it like butter—the chain was nice and new and sharp. I had cut about half a dozen lengths off when I was suddenly splattered by bits of flesh and blood. It scared the living daylights out of me. After I had checked to see if I still had the bottom half of my leg, I saw that I'd completely dismembered a rabbit that had been hiding there. Apparently it had gone as far up the hollow as it could, the end was inevitable. That particular bit of wood is still there; I didn't bother to chuck it into the back of the ute.

Later on I was busy getting stuck into another log when my son got my attention to tell me that there was a bloody great spider crawling up my trouser leg. You have to have your wits about you when playing around with chainsaws—especially when rabbits and spiders take your mind off the job.

Collecting firewood from the bush has many environmental repercussions.

Fallen trees and logs make excellent havens for the likes of rabbits, feral cats and foxes. However they also provide homes for some of our native wildlife before the wood decays and rots away and is ultimately reunited with the soil. That's Nature's cycle.

We are rapidly denuding the place of trees and if the present arborcidal mentality continues we will find ourselves in a treeless world.

Imagine not being able to cut firewood. Imagine a cuddly rabbit being deprived of a home or imagine the poor feral moggy having nowhere to eat its night(ly) parrot!

# Fire and the Australian Bush

Fire caused by lightning and volcanic activity has been an integral part of the Australian environment for at least 350 000 years. Ever since Aborigines first stepped onto Australian shores at least 40 000 years ago they subjected the landscape to a massive systematic burning regime. They used fire for a variety of reasons and it was an essential tool in their daily existence. They depended on it for hunting, cooking and for warmth. It also featured in their spiritual life. These 'firestick farmers' as they have been referred to, had an intimate knowledge of the use and effects of fire. Tribes walked over vast distances burning the country in a mosaic. In 1889 the explorer, Ernest Giles got it right when he recorded 'the natives were about burning, burning, ever burning . . . one would think they lived on fire instead of water'.

Fire was responsible for keeping the balance between the trees, the shrubs and the grasses and maintaining the open parkland appearance that greeted the explorers and early settlers.

With the advent of settlement much of the country in New South Wales soon became what Henry Lawson referred to as 'sheep infested'. Following hard on the hooves of sheep came rabbits, millions and millions of them. They competed with the sheep for grass and ate the country bare. All that remained were the more hardy trees and inedible shrubs. Drought didn't help the situation either. The lack of grass severely decreased the frequency and extent of bushfires and whenever a fire started attempts were made to put it out—just as occurs today.

This has led to major changes in the vegetation over much of Australia.

The once open grazing country with scattered trees and shrubs that lies between the Lachlan and Darling Rivers is now choked with shrubs and little grass. The reasons for these changes go something like this: sheep and rabbits ate the grass, droughts prevented any regrowth, lack of grass reduced fires, shrubs sprang up in the place of grass. Shrubs now dominate the landscape and even after good rain, grass finds the going difficult.

Generally speaking most of the Australian vegetation can cope with fire in one way or another. Probably the most notable exception is rainforest which doesn't burn anyway. The biggest threats to rainforests are logging and clearing for agricultural purposes, but that's another story.

Plants respond to fire in a number of different ways. Some are killed but regenerate from seed. This is common in most acacias, or wattles. Indeed, fire actually promotes the germination of these seeds, and young seedlings emerge in huge numbers following the passage of fire. Other plants merely resprout from their stems or rootstocks. This is how the majority of eucalypts cope with fire.

There is considerable controversy about burning or not burning. Some argue that regular burning-off is necessary to avoid raging wildfires in our hardwood forests and national parks. Others maintain that no deliberate burning should be the rule.

The whole question of burning or not burning and other things like logging or not logging and grazing or not grazing is complex. We have to have sheep, we have to grow crops, we have to have forests and we have to have wood. The real issue is that we have to strike a proper balance between all these and other land uses and we have to know how to manage the land for any one or a mixture of these purposes. We have to maintain a balance between conservation and utilisation.

# Moreton Bay Fig

*Ficus macrophylla*

What do Sydney's Port Jackson and Brisbane's Moreton Bay have in common? The answer is they both have trees named after them—fig trees. The better-known one is the Moreton Bay fig (*Ficus macrophylla*)—*Ficus* because it's a fig and *macrophylla* because of its large leaves.

There are around forty kinds of fig found in Australia, most of them in the rainforests of the eastern coast. Some however, have been able to survive and adapt to much harsher conditions, and today relict stands of some figs can be found in small oases in the dry centre of our continent, a legacy of ages ago when rainforests covered much of Australia.

The Moreton Bay fig can be a very large tree, often growing fifty metres high with a similar spread of its branches. Most of us would have seen these huge trees as they have been planted in countless parks and gardens all over the place. Some are really great for kids to climb and explore—large, very old trees have lots of secret nooks and crannies. The only problem is that the figs stick to your shoes and make a mess inside the house.

These trees occur naturally along the eastern coastal areas of New South Wales from near Narooma to Moreton Bay in Queensland, hence the common name. They were once planted as avenue and park trees but their massive root systems play havoc with paths, roads and building foundations. In fact one city council in Victoria has banned their planting because of problems with roots damaging the sewerage system. The roots can spread to at least the edge of the canopy but in drier parts of Australia they can spread up to ten times this diameter.

The fruits, which resemble those of the cultivated fig, are about one inch across and purple when ripe. They can be eaten but are fairly dry and not very appetising unless you're a fruit-eating bat or bird. These animals spread the seeds and quite often young seedlings can be seen beginning their life in a crevice or the fork of a branch of another tree.

When I was growing up I remember the magnificent Moreton Bay fig on top of Razorback Hill near Camden, on the outskirts of Sydney. 'While I live I'll grow', said the large sign beside it. That lovely old tree is now gone, (I think it fell victim to vandals), as is Anthony Hordens, once Sydney's largest department store. 'While I live I'll grow' was Anthony Hordens' motto and the Moreton Bay fig was their logo.

# White Cypress Pine

## Callitris glaucophylla

A common tree growing over much of the interior of New South Wales is white cypress pine. It's a small to medium-sized tree that can reach thirty metres in height under ideal conditions. It is an attractive tree with dense foliage, especially when growing in open situations, and the classical pyramidal shape gives rise to its common name. However this is confusing because it is not a member of either the true cypresses or pines of the northern hemisphere.

In Australia there about sixteen species of cypress pines, or to give them their scientific name, *Callitris*. They belong to the group of the most primitive seed plants whose fossil records date back some 350 million years, long before the first appearance of the true flowering plants.

White cypress pine forms extensive forests in parts of southern Queensland, the Pilliga scrub and around the Cobar district of New South Wales but its natural occurrence extends into the other States.

The tree is one of many plants to have increased in density over large tracts of country following European settlement. In fact, after only a decade or two, the spread of the pine in parts of western New South Wales so alarmed many landholders that the New South Wales government appointed a Commission to inquire into the spread of pine and other 'noxious' shrubs. Without a doubt, the major cause of this was the reduced frequency and extent of wildfires once land was taken up for grazing. White cypress pine is easily killed by fire, especially when small, and decreased frequency of fire allowed regeneration to occur over vast areas.

Deterioration of the grazing country in western New South Wales finally forced a Royal Commission and, in 1901, evidence provided by numerous witnesses clearly indicated that the spread of pine was a major factor in reducing the productivity of the country.

One witness stated that when he first went to his station in 1865 'there was a large area of beautiful open country on it—nice ridges, very lightly timbered with box and kurrajong. These ridges are now thickly covered with pine scrub, and have become useless'.

The tree was used extensively in the early days for all manner of buildings. It was easy to work and there was a plentiful supply. Large numbers of timber mills sprang up and white cypress pine provided a valuable building material. The wood is highly resistant to attack by white ants and borers but easily splits if nailed. However early buildings were constructed without the use of nails and examples of these are still fairly common around homesteads and in many country towns.

During spring, huge amounts of pollen are shed by the male cones. As each cone bursts open, streams of pollen are shot into the air and the branches quiver as if moved by passion.

The tree is fairly slow growing and in the early stages is eaten and nibbled by sheep and rabbits. However, it makes an attractive garden specimen and will perform quite well, especially if grown in sandy soil.

Beside its use in buildings it makes excellent fence posts but its properties as firewood leave a lot to be desired as it spits and crackles and sparks and can be quite dangerous if the wood is burnt on an open fire inside your house.

# Coolibah

*Eucalyptus coolabah*

Many of our trees have been the subject of songs, poems, stories and bush yarns and occupy a special place in our heritage. It was Banjo Paterson's swagman who immortalised coolibah when he camped beneath its shade.

The tree known as the DIG tree is a coolibah standing on the bank of Coopers Creek. The word 'DIG' was inscribed on the trunk in 1864 by members of the ill-fated Bourke and Wills expedition. This old coolibah is still standing and quite healthy.

Coolibah is a eucalypt which grows along watercourses and places that are liable to flooding in the dry inland parts of all mainland states except Victoria. It has a number of common names—collaille, yathoo, targoon, narrow-leaved box and jumbul kurleah, to name just a few.

Often they are only small trees but in favourable situations where plenty of water is available they may grow quite large. One such specimen growing in western Queensland is supposed to be nearly twenty metres high with branches spreading some forty metres. It is known as the 'Monkira Monster'.

One of the best ways of distinguishing coolibah is that it has rough box-like bark on the trunk and large branches while the smaller branches are smooth and white.

Coolibah wood is very heavy and hard. Because it is highly resistant to termite attack it makes really good fence posts but it's not used much these days.

Coolibahs in themselves are not particularly spectacular. However, if you add the Paroo, a sunset, reflections on the water and a couple of cold stubbies, then you have all the ingredients of an idyllic setting.

# Red Cedar

*Toona australis*

Australia has very few trees that are deciduous. Perhaps the most notable and famous is the red cedar—once the giant of the rainforests of the eastern coast.

It's been said that, next to gold, red cedar was the greatest lure to the early pioneers. Its exploitation by the cedar cutters last century was so great that the tree is now very rare except in some small inaccessible areas of north Queensland.

Once upon a time this tree grew in the rainforests along the eastern coast from about Ulladulla south of Sydney right up to Atherton in Queensland.

Red cedar was first cut in the Sydney area and as early as 1795 logs were exported to India. However, soon the trees became very scarce and the cedar cutters moved up and down the coast in the hunt to find more.

In the early days the trees were felled by axe, floated down rivers to be sawn and then loaded onto ships and taken to the Sydney market.

The country inland from Byron Bay and Ballina supplied huge amounts of cedar last century. This area was known as 'The Big Scrub' and was the largest tall subtropical rainforest in Australia. However, by the 1890s it was gone. The cedar cutters were followed by land-hungry farmers and soon the destruction was complete. The rainforest gave way to Paspalum.

The red cedar fared no better in Queensland. It was gone from the Moreton Bay district by the middle of last century and soon became scarce further up the coast.

Red cedar is the finest of the Australian cabinet timbers. Its reddish coloured wood is durable and light and easy to work and it comes up beautifully when polished. It was, and still is, highly prized. Just take a look in the antique shops!

Attempts to propagate red cedars in plantations have failed. In such situations the trees are attacked by the cedar tip moth which severely deforms or even kills the trees. In their natural rainforest habitat this did not happen because the trees were scattered and could escape the ravages of the moth.

# Tasmanian Blue Gum

## Eucalyptus globulus

Tasmania is the only State that has a tree as its floral emblem—the Tasmanian blue gum.

It grows into a tall majestic tree reaching upwards of seventy metres (that's over 200 feet) and does best in the south eastern parts but occurs right up the eastern coast. It is also found on Flinders and King Islands in Bass Stait and in some areas in southern Victoria.

This tree, like some of the other eucalypts, is rather peculiar in that the young leaves bear no resemblance to the older leaves.

Juvenile leaves are very broad and are attached directly onto a branch in opposite pairs. They are covered with a silvery blue powder which gives the tree its common name. Mature leaves are completely different. They are shiny dark green, very long and are attached by a stalk. Unlike the young leaves they are arranged alternately along the branch.

Another strange kind of metamorphosis occurs in the small branches. Juvenile leaves are attached to branches that are square in cross-section. On the other hand, adult leaves hang from branches that are round.

The trunk has dark persistent bark on the lower parts but above this it peels off in long strips leaving the branches and upper trunk with a smooth whitish bark. These long strips of bark are particularly important during bushfires. When they catch alight they can be carried miles ahead of the fire front by the wind where they start spot fires. This creates havoc for firefighters.

The Tasmanian blue gum is one of the most widely planted eucalypts overseas. Plantations have been established in many overseas countries including Spain, Portugal, India, Brazil, South Africa and the USA. In the main they have been grown for the production of oil from the leaves but are also used for firewood.

One of its most famous claims to fame has been in the prevention of malaria in Italy. Apparently the monks of a Trappist monastery near Rome too often fell the victim of this disease. When visiting Rome in 1869 the Archbishop of Melbourne took some seeds that were to be planted in an attempt to dry up the nearby swamps. The monks planted hundreds of trees which soon dried up the water and, lo and behold, the mosquitoes which carried the malaria parasite disappeared.

The Tasmanian blue gum doesn't appear to be used very much as the State's floral emblem. Many people probably think that the floral emblem is the humble apple. After all, Tasmania is the 'Apple Isle'.

# Banksia

*Banksia* spp.

May Gibbs' children's stories were centred on characters derived from plants and animals found in the bushland she knew and loved so well. The arch enemies of Snugglepot and Cuddlepie and Bib and Bub were the Banksia men—grotesque, hairy, evil ogres of the Australian bush. These Banksia men were inspired by the cones of the common *Banksia serrata*, or old man banksia, which grows along the east coast from Victoria up into Queensland. It is a medium-sized tree and its thick trunk and generally gnarled appearance give it its common name.

The name *Banksia* honours Sir Joseph Banks, who collected the first specimens at Botany Bay in 1770 during Cook's voyage to Australia. Botanists were so impressed with Banks' plant collections that it was proposed to name the land from which they came 'Banksia'.

There are over seventy different kinds of banksias and they occur only in Australia, except for one which extends to islands to our north. They are distributed around the perimeter of our country and are found in all States. The south west part of Western Australia is the richest area for banksias, with some fifty-eight kinds. None is common to both the east and west of Australia.

They grow best in infertile well-drained soils and range in size from small shrubs to medium-sized trees. One of the tallest is the coast banksia which extends from Victoria well up into Queensland.

Banksias are excellent bird attracting plants. Honeyeaters and lorikeets are partial to the nectar and parrots and cockatoos will eat their fruits. The flowers are pollinated by birds, insects and mammals. Honey possum, pygmy possum and native rats are amongst the mammals that pollinate the flowers.

Fire plays an important role in the continued survival of many of our banksias. In some species, the woody fruits mature and remain closed until fire destroys the plant. The heat generated by the flames causes the fruits to open and only then are the seeds released to fall to the ground. The rich bed of ashes left behind by the fire provides an ideal medium for germination. However, this is not always the case. Some banksias can't regenerate if they are burnt too often.

Banksias rate very highly in the cut flower export market and the cones are sometimes used to make souvenirs. There are hundreds of Banksia Streets, Avenues and Roads in towns and cities across Australia. Queensland has its Banksia Beach, South Australia its Banksia Park, Western Australia its Banksiadale while Banksia is a suburb of Sydney. It is probably only wattle that ranks higher in floral street and place names.

# Trees of ANZAC Day

Next to the Shrine of Remembrance in Melbourne stands a large pine tree—an Aleppo Pine, grown from seed collected by an Australian digger at Gallipoli in 1915.

The rugged limestone hills rising up from the landing places at Gallipoli were originally dotted with these pines as well as other trees including oaks and shrubs such as rosemary. During the Gallipoli campaign most of the trees were destroyed—shattered and blown into oblivion by the fierce bombardments.

On the top of one hill a lone pine remained standing. The 7th Battalion attacked and overcame the Turkish positions on the hill, receiving four Victoria Crosses in the process. This famous action became known as the Battle for Lone Pine. It is reputedly from this sole remaining tree that the seed came from which the pine beside the Shrine of Remembrance was grown.

There are three other Aleppo pines in Victoria which were grown from seeds of the Pine at Gallipoli. One is at the Sisters near Terang, one in the Warrnambool Botanic Gardens and one in the Melbourne suburb of Wattle Park.

During the 1960s, Aleppo pines were planted in places such as Colac, Ballarat and Phillip Island in Victoria. Others have been planted in South Australia and in numerous New South Wales towns including Coonabarabran, Dubbo, Forbes, Wagga, Albury and Deniliquin. A number were planted in the 1930s near the War Memorial in Canberra. Hundreds of these trees once lined the main road on the outskirts of Tocumwal, a small town on the banks of the Murray River in New South Wales. In January 1990 a fierce bushfire swept across the area and unfortunately all the trees were completely destroyed.

Aleppo pine is widespread in the Mediterranean region and was an important timber tree of the ancient Greeks who used it for ship building and as a source of pitch. It is probably also the 'fir tree' of the Old Testament.

Another tree closely allied to the ANZAC is the Gallipoli oak, again a native of the Mediterranean. Acorns from a tree at Gallipoli were brought back and planted in 1916 near Hamilton in the Western District of Victoria. Three others were planted in the grounds of Geelong Grammar School. However, only one of these still survives.

Without a doubt, the plant most associated with ANZAC Day is rosemary—the remembrance plant. It is worn on the lapels of thousands of people on the 25th of April every year.

Rosemary is a small shrub and has a wide range of uses. In Greek and Roman times it was important in religious ceremonies and festivals and was regarded as a symbol of fidelity. Oil obtained from the plant forms an ingredient for *Eau de Cologne* and is used in making various lotions and creams. It is also an antiseptic and insecticide. In the kitchen, rosemary is used to flavour meat dishes.

It is a useful small shrub to grow, does well in full sunlight and thrives in poor alkaline soils. Plants can be grown from cuttings taken in autumn.

# Athel Tree

*Tamarix aphylla*

Blackberries, lantana, Paterson's curse, skeleton weed, rabbits, sparrows, feral cats, pigs and horses, cane toads and red-back spiders—I could go on forever. All these plants and animals have been introduced into Australia either intentionally or by accident and are all pests in one form or another. They can occupy valuable and potentially productive agricultural and pastoral land, compete successfully with our native plants and animals, cause soil erosion, transmit disease or bite while you're on the outside dunny. The costs of attempting to control these and the countless other exotic pests in Australia runs to billions of dollars every year.

One of the latest additions to the list is the athel tree or athel pine or tamarisk as it is sometimes known. Athels were introduced into Australia a relatively short time ago, probably in the 1930s but that's not certain. They can grow up to eight metres under favourable conditions but are usually much smaller. While native to the dry areas of north Africa, Asia Minor and north western India they have been extensively planted as shade trees all over the drier inland parts of Australia. They are extremely common around homesteads, yards and shearing sheds and just about every country town.

Here's the crunch—all the major rivers, especially the Finke, flowing out of the Macdonnell Ranges in central Australia, are experiencing a massive invasion of athels.

The source of the invasion was the seemingly innocuous trees planted during the 1950s at homesteads and dams along the river frontage country. The big floods in 1974 carried seed down the river and the river red gums were replaced by the fast growing, salt tolerant athels. Now, most of the lower reaches of the Finke has large areas of these trees growing in the stream bed as well as on the banks. The situation gets worse each time the river flows. Other rivers in the region, the Palmer, Hugh, Todd, Hale and Ross, likewise are becoming invaded.

These trees are changing the course of the rivers. Nesting sites and food sources for native birds and animals common in river red gum communities have been eliminated. Athels pump large quantities of water from the soil and pass huge amounts of salt through their leaves onto the ground below. As the salt content of the soil beneath the trees builds up the only plants able to grow in such situations are weeds.

In all probability the invasion will continue. The trees have virtually no fodder value and they thrive on saline water. Heaven forbid athels ever getting into Lake Eyre or any of the other salt lakes in the interior.

So far there is no sign of these trees invading other river systems. However the potential is there, especially where trees have been planted close to rivers, creeks and bore drains or anywhere where flooding is likely to occur. If you require shade or want to prevent stream bank erosion then native plants that occur naturally around your area are the go.

# Christmas Bush

*Ceratopetalum gummiferum*   (NSW)
*Prostanthera lasianthos*   (Vic)
*Bursaria spinosa*   (SA and Tas)
*Nuytsia floribunda*   (WA)

Like most common plant names, the term Christmas bush refers to various kinds of plants in different regions and states. In the Sydney area Christmas bush is a small tree growing naturally in infertile soils of forest areas and gullies. Its flowers are a creamy colour but the parts surrounding the flower give it the pinkish red colour that makes it so attractive. This particular plant is interesting because it is a remnant from a period some fifty million years ago when rainforest extended across southern Australia, and it is closely related to the coachwood of the rainforests further north. It is also one of the few rainforest trees to have adapted to the low fertility sandy soils around Sydney.

The Victorian Christmas bush is related to the mintbushes and is more of a shrub than a tree. In summer it has masses of snowy white flowers and can be found along creek banks in moist gullies near Melbourne and the Dandenongs. Young saplings of this shrub are highly prized by boys for making fishing rods.

The South Australian Christmas bush is yet another species called by this common name. It is a densely branched shrub or small tree, quite spiny, and has numerous creamy flowers during summer. This Christmas bush grows in almost all parts of the State but is more common in the south east of South Australia, especially in association with mallee.

If you live in the West then you have the Western Australian Christmas tree. It's a shrub or small tree growing to about seven metres high with attractive orange and yellow flowers in summer. It is one of the most beautiful of our native trees and grows on well drained soils from the Murchison River right around to the Bight. The tree is parasitic on the roots of other plants and is related to the mistletoes. In its natural habitat it sends its underground stems out for hundreds of metres in search of host plants from which it gains the nutrients essential for its survival.

# Australia's Floral Emblem

What's got 'little balls of yellow fluff'? The answer of course is golden wattle, *Acacia pycnantha*, our national floral emblem.

The push for a national floral emblem started last century, in 1899 in fact. A bloke in Victoria began a Wattle Club and wanted to promote a wattle day every September to encourage its acceptance as a symbol of patriotism. Public fervour was at an all-time high. The Boer War, a new century and the approach of Federation in 1901 were the ingredients of this new nationalism.

However, the patriotic wave ebbed and it wasn't until around 1910 that the swell for a wattle day again gained momentum. By 1912 New South Wales, South Australia, Victoria and Queensland all recognised Wattle Day.

Even so, New South Wales fought for the waratah as the national flower. However at the suggestion of the South Australian Branch, the Australia Day Wattle League selected golden wattle as the national flower. I'm not sure exactly when this was but it was certainly prior to the outbreak of war in 1914.

The controversy over whether the waratah or wattle was given the semi-official nod was highlighted when both were depicted on the spades used by the VIPs when laying the Foundation Stone for the founding of Canberra in 1913.

Golden wattle has masses of brilliant yellow flowerheads and long leathery leaves. It is often a rather straggly small tree or shrub which is found in open woodland country of southern New South Wales, Victoria and South Australia. Like other wattles it regrows from seed after a fire and can form fairly dense thickets. It stands up to frosts reasonably well and can be grown in just about any soil.

The bark of golden wattle contains a large amount of tannin and was once used extensively as a source of tanbark for use in the tanning of leather. Early settlers even prepared an extract from the bark as a bush cure for diarrhoea.

When I was at school Wattle Day was the first of August but others claim that it's the first of September. Perhaps the beginning of September would be best. After all, it's the start of spring and most wattles are in their prime flowering period then.

# Wattle

*Acacia* spp.

There are more types of wattle, or, more correctly, acacia in Australia than there are gum trees—all up, about 750 different species. They occur naturally in just about every corner of our continent, from Mt. Kosciusko, to the coast, the rainforests and the hot desert parts of the interior.

They range in size from small ground-hugging shrubs only a couple of inches high to fairly large trees—the tallest being a toss-up between the blackwood of Tassie and Victoria and the marblewood which grows in the rainforests of northern New South Wales and southern Queensland.

Acacias are a very old group of plants. They first appeared some 120 million years ago when Australia, Africa, India, South America and Antarctica were all joined in one supercontinent called Gondwanaland.

Unlike many of the acacias of other countries ours don't have prickly spines or thorns. Obviously there are exceptions but on the whole they are free of these nasties— an interesting lesson in adaptation to environmental influences and probably something to do with the fact that the Australian acacias evolved in the absence of large herbivores that fed on them.

The acacias have developed various adaptations and strategies that have enabled them to survive and reproduce in a range of harsh and inhospitable climatic conditions.

They have their own method of overcoming the inherently low fertility of our soils. Their fine roots are covered with small nodules that contain bacteria. These very specialised microscopic bugs actually convert the nitrogen in the air into a form the plant can feed on.

Fierce bushfires don't pose any threat to acacias. Even though most fires will kill the plant they have the ability to either sucker from their roots or regenerate from seed. Seeds that lie dormant in the soil are cracked by the heat of a fire. This then lets moisture into the seed and so the germination process can begin. It is quite common to see massive numbers of Acacia seedlings popping up all over the place after a fire. The success or otherwise of the plants is then dependent upon enough follow-up rain and not being devoured by sheep or rabbits.

The hard wood of some wattles was used by Aborigines for making various implements such as boomerangs, shields, spears and digging sticks. The seeds of some inland species were ground into flour before being cooked and eaten. Wooden ornaments made from the wood, especially mulga, must rank next to toy koalas among the typically Australian souvenirs favoured by tourists.

One kind of wattle known as mimosa bush or prickly moses is cultivated in some Mediterranean countries for the production of Oil of Cassie, an expensive ingredient of perfumes.

Acacias in one form or another have provided everything from food to fuel, fibre and fence posts. However, not all are that good to have around.

In the normally treeless Mitchell grass country of Queensland, prickly Acacia has overrun more than six million hectares, that's about fifteen million acres, of valuable grazing land. This particular Acacia was introduced from the Middle East early this century and was planted along bore drains, presumably to provide shade for stock. So successful has its invasion been that it is now a declared noxious weed.

Another Acacia, known as kangaroo thorn, has been declared a noxious plant in Victoria owing to its uninviting sharp thorns and its capacity to spread quickly. However, unlike the introduced prickly Acacia, the latter is native to Australia.

Wattles are undoubtedly one of our most spectacular flowering plants. In the main their blossoms are yellow but vary from almost white to orange. There is even one particular type that occurs in northern Queensland and has purple flowers. The common names of some wattles often don't give a clue that they are indeed wattles. However I reckon that names like dead finish, wait-a-while, currawang, yarran, nelia and gundabluey are much better than unimaginative names such as grey wattle, silver wattle, prickly wattle and hairy wattle.

Wattle's praises have been sung and written about by numerous people. Henry Lawson wrote about it in his patriotic war poem *Waratah and Wattle*. The Bullamakanka band have since put it to music. John Williamson sings about Cootamundra wattle and how it brings back memories.

The Australian use of the word 'wattle' is purely local practice. In many countries the flowers are called 'mimosa', as Australians have found in the flower markets of London and Europe. It's usually believed that the word 'wattle' came from the type of saplings used by the early settlers to make wattle and daub huts. On the other hand, the word 'wattah' is given by several early writers in New South Wales as an Aboriginal word for wattle.

Whatever the origin, the name is recognised by all Australians, and the green and gold colours are synonymous with the outfits of Allan Border and his mates, the boxing kangaroo and our Olympic Games teams.

Wattle flowers produce no nectar for honey but bees are attracted to the large amounts of sweetly scented pollen. Wattle blossoms can even be used in cooking. For something different, try them in fritters. Strip the flowers from the stems and mix into a light batter before frying—they go well with a bit of sugar and whipped cream or Golden Syrup. For a truly Australian snack the flowers can be added to the mixture before cooking pikelets.